FOR KEYBOARDS

by

WILLIAM T. EVELETH

ISBN 978-0-7935-2091-6

HAL•LEONARD®
CORPORATION
7777 W. BLUEMOUND RD. P.O. BOX 13819 MILWAUKEE, WI 53213

FOR

Barbara,

Mom and Dad,

and Charlotte

BLUES, JAZZ, & ROCK RIFFS *for* KEYBOARDS

Contents

Introduction

Blues, Jazz and Rock Riffs for Keyboards presents a practical approach to improvising through a system of traditional blues patterns. These "riffs and licks" are a varied collection of well known phrases and figures. They are widely used by experienced players of most any style that has a characteristic "bluesy" sound. Because so much of today's popular music ultimately traces its roots back to the original blues, the material included here is a vital component of jazz, rock and roll, R & B, New Orleans, gospel, soul, boogie-woogie, and, for that matter, much of today's pop music.

Ironically, despite the immense popularity of these styles, a great deal of this music has never been written down. Sheet music is usually available, but it rarely reflects more than a trace of the artists' stylistic idioms, with solo passages generally omitted. Fortunately, in recent years, publishers have increasingly offered transcriptions. Nevertheless, musicians wanting to develop their own authentic "sound" in these styles still must learn what they can, either from teachers and other players or by making their own painstaking transcriptions.

A number of excellent books are available that explain the theoretical aspects of improvisation. These books teach us everything we could possibly want to know about scales, modes, voicings, rhythm, and so on. But in my view, knowing the blues scale does not a blues player make. Something critical is missing, the answers to the questions all musicians have wanted to ask at one time or another when they watch a good player perform: "What did you just play? Could you teach me that?"

What you will find in *Blues, Jazz and Rock Riffs for Keyboards* is my attempt to document some of the "stuff" that good piano blues are made of — the actual licks, riffs, cadences, embellishments, and basic patterns that define the style. I have tried to assemble a collection of figures that is as complete and typical as possible, but with a slight preference for right-hand lines with more than one voice, that is, using two or more fingers simultaneously. Single voice patterns — which seem to be well covered in books for horn players — don't adequately reflect either the true range of expression of the piano or the idiomatic way it is played.

For the record, much of the material presented here is drawn from the playing of influential artists whose music spans many styles:

Albert Ammons
Ray Charles
"Fats" Domino
Vince Guaraldi
James P. Johnson
Pete Johnson
Meade Lux Lewis
"Dr. John" MacRebennack
"Jelly Roll" Morton
Oscar Peterson
Memphis Slim
Art Tatum
"Fats" Waller
Teddy Wilson
Jimmy Yancey

Yet, few of the melodic figures in

Blues, Jazz and Rock Riffs for Keyboards can, or should, be attributed to a particular artist. They are part of the "common knowledge" of the blues legacy which has been passed from one player to the next, modified slightly, or over time adapted to a new style. The composers and players listed above are undoubtedly an excellent source for authentic material. Still, one could just as well put together a similar collection of patterns based on the playing of an entirely different set of artists. In fact, a good many of the "classic" examples presented here have been selected from a variety of recent tunes, including top hits from groups and artists like Fine Young Cannibals, the Pointer Sisters, Madonna, Miami Sound Machine, and Harry Connick, Jr.

I have assembled as comprehensive a collection of blues figures as possible, recognizing that one can only hope to capture a limited sampling of the richness and variety of this art form. Anyway, the blues style should never be thought of as simply a collection of riffs and licks. I hope that the major benefit you get out of working with a collection like this is to develop, through exposure to a great number of illustrative examples, your own "feel" for the style. Therefore, when you play these figures, I recommend that you pay close attention to the rhythmic structures, the harmonic progressions, and the voicings.

To help you do this, whenever possible, the patterns have been arranged by structure as well as by musical function. Additionally, theoretical explanations and general concepts are provided to enable you to develop your own interesting figures.

After every few chapters you will find short pieces that illustrate how these figures are actually used in typical blues, jazz, and rock styles.

With one or two exceptions, all of the patterns are presented in the Key of C. This has been done to simplify memorization, comparison, and transposition to other keys. For the same reasons, figures are generally written within a few octaves of middle C. However, in order to maximize your facility with them, I strongly recommend that you practice and learn the patterns in several keys.

For example, you can start out by learning a few of your favorite patterns in the keys of C, F, and G. You will then be prepared to improvise with them through a traditional 12-bar blues progression like the one presented in the section, "Chord Changes." These patterns should also be practiced in the higher registers, where many of them are often played and are especially effective.

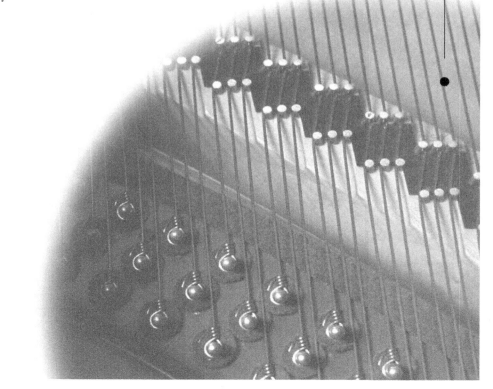

Classic Blues Licks

Let's start with a collection of classic licks. Licks are short, often flashy, phrases used for embellishment or as fillers. Some of these are so popular you can hear them practically everywhere. The first one, for example, is used as a riff, or repeated theme, in countless tunes. It may well have been first played as a rock variation of the second example, a boogie-woogie figure.

Many of these licks are extracted from longer passages. Rather than leave them as incomplete fragments, I have added simple resolutions. You can play them as written or else skip the last note or chord and continue with your own improvisation. In fact, you may want to consider these figures no more than a starting point for creating your own original licks.

Embellishments

Grace notes, or slides, are an essential feature of the blues sound. They also appear in most jazz, rock, boogie, and pop styles. Be sure to note the many different ways they are used to create interesting effects in the patterns in this book. A few examples of typical figures and chords with grace notes follow:

It is important to use the fingering indicated on these ornaments so that you can play them without stumbling or feeling awkward. Unlike classical technique, in blues playing, the same finger is generally used on the grace note as on the note that follows. The effect is intentionally less precise. In fact, the grace note should "blur" into the second. This creates an approximation of tones from the true blues scale that cannot actually be played on the piano since they fall in between the half-tone step of two adjacent keys. By using fewer fingers, you also free up the rest of your hand for greater mobility and speed.

This fingering system applies when sliding from a black to a white key but obviously cannot be used to go from white to white or from white to black. In these cases, use two fingers and try to bring about the same sound achieved with one sliding finger.

Blues players commonly use two or even three grace notes in a row. The first example below is a very popular blues figure.

Because the volume diminishes rapidly after a note is played on the piano, even when the sustain pedal is used, *tremolos* are often used to extend the length of duration of chords. They are also frequently used in blues styles purely for their coloristic effect.

Teddy Wilson—like many other jazz players—frequently played short tremolos on the octave (first example below). The second example is a classic blues figure: a tremolo on a minor third, embellished with a double grace note.

Tremolos also make great introductions, as used in the styles of "Pine Top" Smith and Meade Lux Lewis. In his introductions, Lewis builds up the energy to a high level with a two-handed tremolo that he sustains throughout the rest of the number with his famous driving boogie bass line. This tremolo is a little tricky to play but a good exercise in hand coordination.

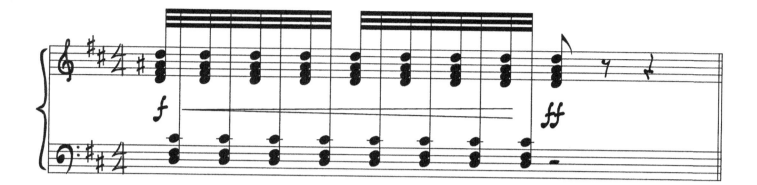

Here is a final example, another tremolo played by alternating hands. It is one of the many trademarks of "Fats" Waller.

Trills are occasionally used in jazz:

And another important device used to create more interesting lines is to replace a simple eighth note pattern (A) with an embellished *turn* such as (B). Oscar Peterson frequently plays this kind of figure.

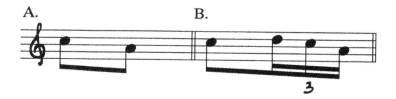

"Lead-in's"

One element common to many blues licks is the "lead-in"—the short runs that are found at the beginning of many patterns. Like grace notes, they are a form of embellishment, but are longer, usually three to five notes. As you play through the examples, notice how much these "lead-in's" contribute to the overall blues sound.

A number of typical lead-in's are shown below. They are based on either ascending, as in the first set, or descending scales, usually pentatonic, blues, or chromatic. Note as well the many varied rhythmic constructions used.

Ascending lead-in's

Descending lead-in's

Here are some excellent licks containing lead-in's like those played by Dr. John, Harry Connick, Jr., Jimmy Yancey, and others. Because several of these are fragments from solo passages, you may want to develop them into more complete, original lines of your own.

Group 1 Ascending

Group 2 Descending

Arpeggios

Arpeggios are an essential feature in blues piano lines. You'll find them at the heart of many classic licks where they add rhythmic interest and texture. The examples given here are short figures chosen to show some of the many ways they are used.

A simple, repeated broken chord is a good way to maintain the rhythm in the right hand:

You can also create embellishments from chord tones to add interest, as in the example below:

Longer sequences of chord tones, especially runs of 4, 5, or 6 notes, help create passages with rhythmic variety. Several excellent blues licks containing arpeggios follow. As you play through them, notice the many rhythmic variations that arpeggios are commonly played in.

Many of these examples are classic blues licks for your repertoire. In the last example, the first four notes make up an important pattern that is frequently heard in blues passages. A few common variations on it are shown below:

Boogie Bass Lines

Even if boogie-woogie is not your favorite style, I strongly recommend that you learn at least a few of the standard boogie bass lines because they are so widely used in blues, rock and roll, R&B, New Orleans, pop styles, and, occasionally, even in jazz.

Boogie bass figures create the driving effect characteristic of rhythmic styles like rock. They therefore must be played with a very steady beat. Any disruption of the rhythm will spoil the intended effect.

Many of these bass lines are quite difficult to play and may take considerable practice to master. The goal is to develop independence in the left hand, because an even greater challenge comes when you try to add a right hand part. Keep your left hand steady but relaxed and be as economical as possible with your motion, otherwise tightening of the wrist may result.

One excellent way to develop your skill with these figures is to practice away from the piano, by playing them on your thighs or on a table. If you have limited time available to spend at the keyboard, you can get a lot of tedious practice done whenever you would otherwise find yourself killing time, waiting in line or driving, for example.

Start with one or two of these bass figures that you find easy to play. Practice playing them (with the left hand alone) through various chord changes and with as steady a rhythm as possible. Then try to learn other bass figures the same way. Eventually you want to be able to switch freely from one pattern to another, always keeping the beat steady. After you've developed a palette of left hand figures that you can play independently, you will have an excellent basis for a free-wheeling improvisation in the right hand.

The bass lines included here are written as a mixture of straight and "swinging" or "shuffling" rhythms. It is common practice to write in straight eighth notes (A) when they are intended and understood to be played with a swinging feel (B). Dotted eighths are also sometimes used to approximate the effect.

Consider all of these figures open to modification according to your own preference. In some cases, a perfectly straight rhythm might be the effect you are looking for.

"Hey, Good Lickin'" brings together a handful of the classic blues licks that you have learned so far: arpeggios, lead-in runs, and a few different boogie bass lines. Also note the use of grace notes and tremolos. You will find nearly all of the material for this number in the previous sections. The piece ends with what is known as a cadence. These are discussed in the next section.

HEY, GOOD LICKIN'

BILL EVELETH

Blues Cadences

Cadences are short harmonic progressions played at the end of a phrase to clearly signal its end and, often, the beginning of the next phrase. I've selected a few of the most commonly used blues-style cadences and some interesting variations on them. Most of these cadences are written as endings. Add the V7 chord when a new section will follow, as shown in the second example below.

Probably the single most popular of all blues cadences, the following progression (shown in a simplified form) is truly a classic:

A good way to remember this useful progression is to keep in mind the descending parallel sixths formed by the internal voices. Here are some typical variations on this progression:

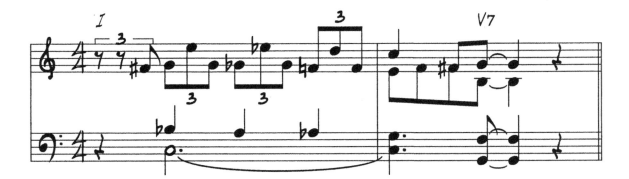

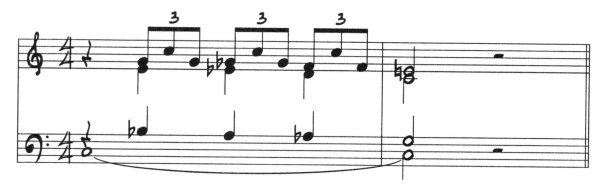

And here are several other cadences based on various other progressions:

The following progressions are also the basis for many popular blues cadences. As an exercise, try to develop your own cadences based on them.

The progressions in this section illustrate an important technique for developing well-constructed, harmonically logical blues phrases. Start with a short, simple progression of two-note chords. A series of about four such chords in a chromatic or other scale sequence generally works quite well. The next step is to develop a riff by embellishing the underlying chords with grace notes, arpeggios, and lead-in runs, just as you have done in the preceding sections.

Here are several examples of the types of progressions that could be used to develop blues riffs. Notice that some of these are simply ascending or descending parallel sixths, which work well in parallel constructions. (We'll come back to this in the section, "The Sound of Fourths.")

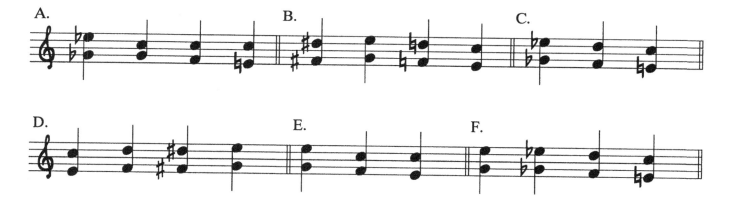

And here are few figures based on these progressions:

B.

C.

D.

E.

F.

Patterns in Thirds

With the major exception of bebop, which primarily favors single-note playing reminiscent of horn lines, nearly all piano styles make extensive use of multi- as well as single-voice lines. Blues patterns based on major and minor thirds are especially common and contribute to the characteristic sound, or texture, of many styles. If you're not accustomed to playing "in thirds," you may find that the patterns in this section will add a new dimension to your style. The examples here include versatile standard progressions that can be heard in many kinds of music.

As we'll see in "Chord Changes," standard blues progressions are based on dominant seventh chords. The same harmonies also add to the "bluesy" character of jazz, rock, and the many other styles that trace their origins to the blues. For this reason, a scale of thirds built on the intervals of the dominant seventh chord is an excellent basis for improvising in these styles.

And here are some of the most common sequences upon which blues patterns are based:

Keeping these simplified progressions in mind should help you create typical blues, jazz, boogie, and rock patterns of your own. But first, let's see how some of the best players create riffs and licks out of these patterns. Generally, other "blue" notes besides the flatted seventh, namely the flatted third and flatted fifth, are also added to create chromatic passages, of which the following examples are typical:

Two other important patterns are:

Before we proceed to the figures, I'd like to point out one more basic blues sequence, in simplified form:

It is typical in the blues style to harmonize the tonic note (in this case, C in the first chord) with the fourth below (G). If we were to use a third here (that is, C with the A below it), the harmony would suggest an F or an A minor chord. This does not present a problem in a passing sequence, but would not be desirable when you wish to support the underlying harmony of a C chord. For this reason, many of the patterns in this section are based on the following set of chords:

Undoubtedly, you will find among the following patterns some choice licks for your repertoire. Beyond that, as you play through these examples you should begin to get a feel for the technique.

36

The last example (B), is an interesting variation of a well-known boogie riff (A), with some of the thirds played as arpeggios.

A.

B.

Adding Harmonic Notes to Melodic Lines

Here is an excellent technique for creating fuller, more harmonically interesting right hand lines. It is highly versatile—you'll find it in figures throughout this book—and the sound is characteristic of not only blues but other styles as well, including country music. Virtually all the top pianists use this technique in their improvising. And you may be surprised how effective and easy it is.

In its simplest form, the basic idea is as follows:

The trick is to add harmony to your improvised (melodic) line by playing a second voice made up of the tonic of the chord on which you are improvising. As you play, repeat the closest tonic note above the melody with each note of the melody.

For example, if your improvised line were a descending C major scale played on the chord change of C major, you would play the following:

Similarly, you would harmonize a descending blues line as follows:

Here are a few more examples of figures created in this way:

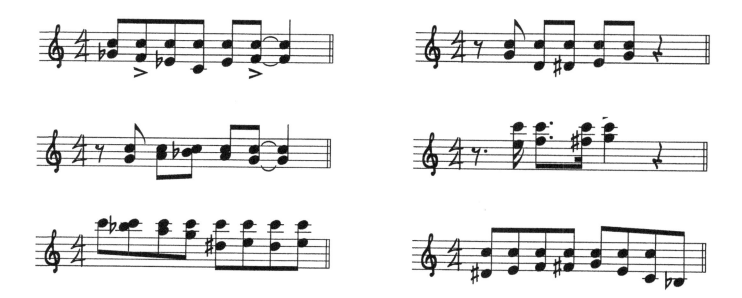

Notice in the last example that the top voice is dropped on the last note to add variety to the texture. This leads us to some variations on this technique.

Variation 1: To create an even more interesting passage, alternate between a harmonized and a single-note melody line, in some cases adding the second voice only sparingly. As you play the examples below, notice that the harmonic voice can also be tied instead of repeated.

In the next example, a fairly simple melodic theme is developed into a driving solo with a funky syncopated rhythm. The texture is created by the theme moving against the harmonic voice, which stays put on the tonic. Alternation between single notes and octaves on the the tonic creates the desired percussive effect. You'll learn more about this last device later.

Variation 2: The tonic is the most common and the easiest note to add without producing undesired dissonances, because it simply reinforces the underlying harmony. However, you can also harmonize by using other scale tones, such as the third, fifth, or sixth.

Several examples using these other tones follow. As you play through them, keep in mind that they are all written to go with a C chord (unless stated otherwise). Experiment using C7 and Cmin chords or else a C note in the bass. Also try playing these figures in different keys and registers.

In the first example, notice how someone like Oscar Peterson might create a blues effect by embellishing the melody (A) with grace notes and adding the fifth on the second chord change (B).

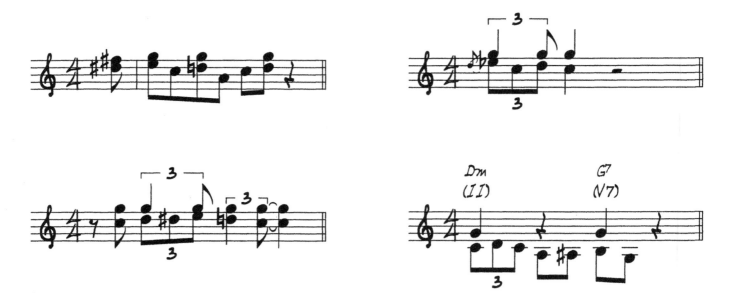

In the last example, the same harmonic note is maintained through a chord change. This particular figure shows up in the improvisations of many of the best jazz players.

Variation 3: You can create a similar sound by adding the harmonic voice below your lead line. This structure is less frequently heard, however.

As an exercise, play through the examples to develop familiarity with the concept. Several of the figures presented are "standards" and can be heard in the solo work of many different artists. Some are worth adding to your own blues vocabulary. As you gain a feel for the technique, you will find that you can add harmonic notes to your own improvised lines automatically, without being conscious of the intervals you are selecting. The main point is to add harmonic interest and texture by introducing a second, fixed voice.

"Sweet Talk" is a short jazz tune that illustrates some of the concepts we have explored in the last few sections. At the beginning, licks with one fixed and one moving voice are featured. In the last few bars you will find a few patterns in thirds. The piece ends with a lick similar to the ones described at the end of the section, "Blues Cadences."

SWEET TALK

BILL EVELETH

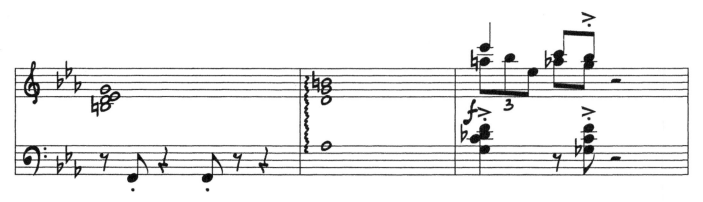

Classic Runs

Nearly all styles make use of runs of one form or another. In terms of structure, the simplest, but also among the most difficult to play well, are those based on descending pentatonic scales:

Elegant linear runs of this sort are especially prevalent in the stride styles of jazz players like Art Tatum and Teddy Wilson. They must be played evenly and legato.

The other type of run in this chapter is commonly used by blues, rock and roll, and R&B players. This second kind is more rhythmic and should be played somewhat percussively.

Finally, you will encounter in the figures presented here some excellent licks that technically are not runs as such but, as patterns that are repeated in descending octaves, have a similar construction.

44

Play It Again

Repetition is one of the most important and easiest ways to improvise. Yet this device is rarely covered in depth in books on improvisation, which typically stress more advanced concepts, such as the "locrian mode" or "extended dominants." It may be that repetition is considered too obvious and therefore unnecessary to explain. In my view, it deserves at least some coverage here because not only is it an essential element of strongly rhythmic styles like rock and roll and boogie-woogie, but the best jazz players also make liberal use of this device.

Virtually any figure can be repeated as the basis for an improvisation. However, there are a number of patterns that are especially suited to repetition and worth noting here because of their widespread use in this way. I've tried to select classic patterns for you to add to your repertoire.

Many of us think of the piano primarily for its melodic and harmonic qualities. These patterns bring out the percussive nature of the instrument. They are written in the key of C and are intended to be played along with a C chord, generally Cmaj, Cmin, or C7. Many of them also work well when played through harmonic changes. For example, you can keep repeating the same notes in the right hand as the harmonic progression (your left hand or the group you're playing with) moves to the IV chord (F) or to the V chord (G).

A. Unisons and Octaves

B. Thirds

C. Fourths

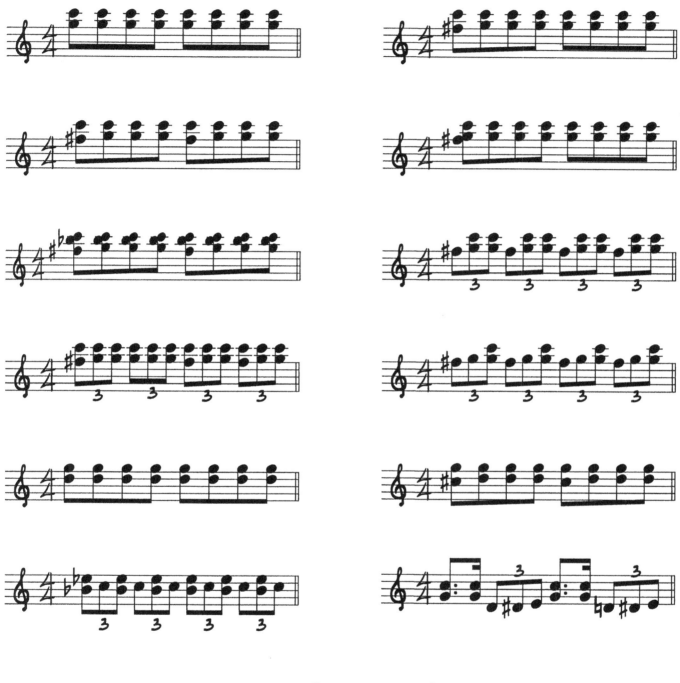

48

D. Fifths

E. Sixths

F. Miscellaneous Chords

You can also create driving motion with chords played in rhythms that contrast with the underlying beat:

G. Linear Patterns

You can create interesting effects by playing a three-note pattern in a four-note rhythm, and vice versa. Even more elaborate effects result when a second voice is added in contrasting rhythm:

H. Other Miscellaneous Patterns

The Power of Octaves

Playing in octaves contributes greatly to a professional sound—not only in the blues, but in most any style. You can play either straight octaves in the right hand, or else play parallel lines in both hands. Both devices are especially useful to increase the piano's volume when playing in a group.

Here are a few examples to illustrate the effects that you can create. First, try playing the same line in both hands a few octaves apart. The bars below may remind you of Oscar Peterson:

The use of octaves in both hands is also an important element of the Latin dance band sound. In this example, notice the alternation between octaves and arpeggios in a syncopated rhythm. This passage is similar to the piano solos used by groups like Miami Sound Machine. You can hear similar playing in many other recordings.

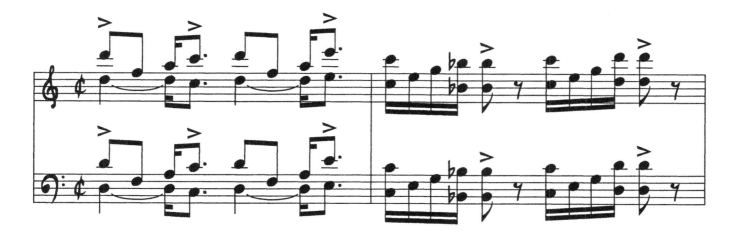

Here are two other typical Latin dance figures using parallel, syncopated lines in the right and left hands.

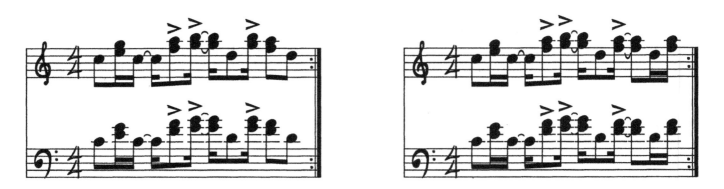

When you play early rock and roll, Kansas City boogie-woogie, or other styles based on straight eighth notes in 4/4 time, you can use repeating octaves on scale patterns or on one note to keep the time. This device is excellent for introductions, fillers, and turnarounds.

Jazz players also commonly use octave chords to punctuate the rhythm in a bell effect:

A final important concept concerning the effective use of octaves is that of alternation. Some rock and roll players, Leon Russell for example, are known for long percussive passages of straight octaves. However, players of less intense styles more typically try to create lines that mix octaves and single notes. The resulting texture combines the benefits of the volume and percussiveness of the octaves and the greater speed that can be achieved with single-notes:

"Monkey Girl," a rock and roll number, kicks off with a flashy blues run. Look for repeated figures and patterns in thirds and octaves. In the last bar the harmonic progression is from G to C. Chord changes is the subject of the next section.

MONKEY GIRL

BILL EVELETH

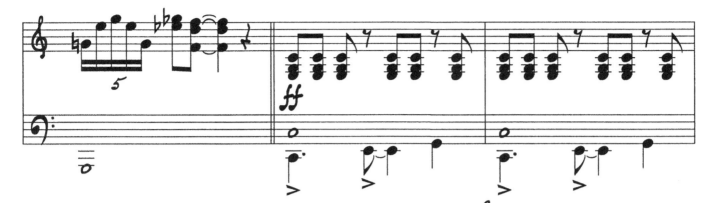

Chord Changes

Experienced players keep in their bags of tricks a number of short phrases that provide smooth, musically logical, and in-rhythm transitions through common chord changes. Included in this section is a collection of some of the better known and most popular figures used for this purpose.

The fundamental structure of the standard blues progression, and indeed of much popular music, involves movement from the tonic (I), to the fourth (IV), back to the tonic (I), down a fourth to the dominant (V), and back to the tonic. You can see this below in the harmonic structure of a basic 12-bar blues progression, which could apply to many rock and roll or R&B numbers as well:

Harmony: I | I | I | I | IV | IV | I | I | V | V | I | I |
Measure: 1 | 2 | 3 | 4 | 5 | 6 | 7 | 8 | 9 | 10 | 11 | 12 |

In the Key of C, the following changes would be used:

Chords: C7 | C7 | C7 | C7 | F7 | F7 | C7 | C7 | G7 | G7 | C7 | C7 |

The figures in this chapter are presented in two groups corresponding to harmonic progressions like the one above. Use the Group 1 progressions when the harmony moves up a fourth (as in bar 4, where the progression changes from the I to the IV chord—in this case to an F7 chord in the Key of C). Use figures from Group 2 when the harmony moves down a fourth or up a fifth (as in bar 8).

You can also use any of the figures from Group 2 in bar 6, because the progression from IV back to I is also a change down a fourth.

The "Circle of Fifths" neatly illustrates the fact that if we move from the tonic (I) to the fourth (IV), or fifth (V), and then continue to repeat the process, we will eventually find ourselves back where we first started. We know from basic music theory that the progression from the V chord to the I chord (counter clockwise on the diagram) is one of the most fundamental and logical progressions in music. Any of the Group 1 figures will bring about a harmonic change in this direction, and will, therefore, prove especially useful for effecting chord changes that make musical sense.

Circle of Fifths

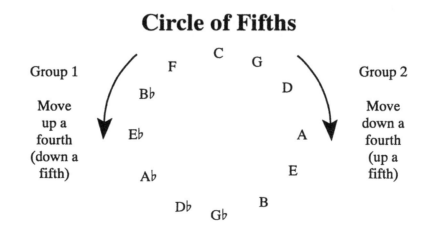

Group 1: Moving Up a Fourth

The patterns in this set correspond to a chord change up a fourth, most commonly from I to IV (or from V to I). As with other examples in this book, they are written in the Key of C but will ideally be learned in several keys.

Several of these phrases follow, at least partially, the simple progression of parallel sixths shown below. Knowing this may help you commit some of the examples to memory and create your own variations.

To add musical interest, this progression is further modified in some of the examples by inserting other sixth chords at chromatic intervals. These are shown in brackets:

Here are the actual patterns, which are used by a number of different players of various styles. You may find these examples suitable for your own style or as a starting point for creating new versions of your own. In the first example, note the use of broken sixth chords.

In the next two examples the sixth chord is replaced by a run starting on the C, going to the A♭, and returning to the C. The effect is highly characteristic of the blues and is widely used by many of the best jazz players as well.

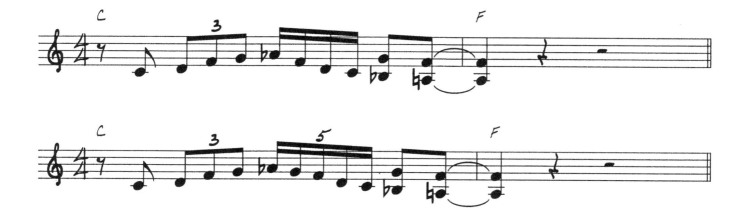

A second sequence useful for moving up a fourth is the chromatic scale:

And here are a few typical patterns based on this idea:

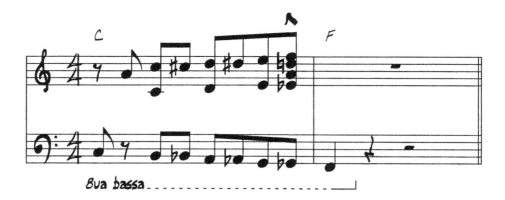

8va bassa _

Group 2: Moving Down a Fourth

The patterns in this group will take you down a fourth, usually from the I chord to the V chord, or from IV back to I. Like their counterparts in Group 1, some of these figures are based on a sequence of descending parallel sixths:

This progression, and variations on it are the basis for the following classic blues figures:

Another I to V (or IV to I) sequence that frequently appears in blues progressions is shown below:

A typical riff based on this progression illustrates its effectiveness:

The Sound of Fourths

One of the challenges piano players face when they want to play simple harmonic structures in the right hand instead of single-note passages is finding the best intervals to add below the melody. The most common intervals used in the patterns we've seen so far are thirds, sixths, and octaves. One reason for this is that two-note chords on these intervals work well in parallel constructions, that is, where the same interval is constantly used to create harmony throughout a passage.

To convince yourself of this, try harmonizing a descending scale on C7, for example, with various intervals added below. Notice how well octaves, thirds, and sixths (which are actually inverted thirds) agree with the underlying chord:

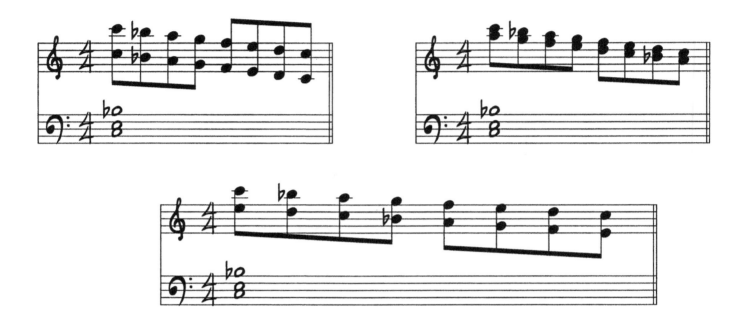

Now try the same with fourths. In this case many of the sonorities created are either dissonant or not what we normally expect to hear in traditional blues harmony.

Even though fourths may be less versatile than some of the other intervals in parallel constructions, their characteristic sound makes them indispensable components of any style that is said to be well-balanced and varied in texture.

On the following page is a collection of figures chosen to illustrate some of the ways to build interesting phrases around the interval.

Fourths also make good "chop" chords. These are chords played percussively to reinforce the rhythm, as in:

More Classic Riffs and Licks

Here's an assorted collection of figures from some of the great blues, jazz, and R&B players, ranging from simple patterns to short phrases.

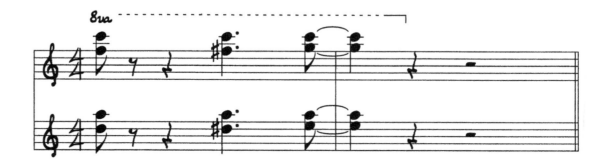

"L. A. Baby" starts out as a slow blues tune. The second section has a swinging feel with a walking bass line. The piece contains figures from throughout this book, particularly from the last few sections. Note the licks played on chord changes, patterns in fourths, and figures from the last chapter, including the Count Basie–style ending.

L.A. BABY

BILL EVELETH